*For the most stylish
girl I know . . .*

....

PRODUCTION

Armelle Saint-Mleux
Olga Sekulic

Benoît Peverelli
Photographer

Rodolphe Bricard
Photographic Assistant

Laura de Lucia
Digital Operator

Jeanne Le Bault
Stylist

Marie-Aline Boussagnol
Stylist Assistant

Marielle Loubet
Hair and Makeup

Elisabeth Serve and Sabine Cayet
Flat Lay Stylists

Marla at Marilyn Agency
Model

Studio Rouchon

Stephane Neme
Set Assistant

Workingirl / Johanna Scher
Production

Jennifer Soulhac
Production Coordinator

Jean-Louis Bergamini
General Manager

Alexandra Kan
Studio Manager

FLAMMARION

Julie Rouart
Editorial Director, French edition

Pierre-Yann Lallaizon
Designer

English edition

Kate Mascaro
Editorial Director

Helen Adedotun
Editor

Jeanne B. Cheynel
Translator

Barbara Jaegy
Production

Bussière, Paris
Color Separation

Printed in Spain by Indice

Originally published in French as
*Comment je m'habille aujourd'hui:
Le style de la Parisienne*
© Flammarion, S.A., Paris, 2016

English-language edition
© Flammarion, S.A., Paris, 2017

editions.flammarion.com

17 18 19   3 2 1

ISBN: 978-2-08-020227-7

Legal Deposit: 04/2017

INES DE LA FRESSANGE
SOPHIE GACHET

PARISIAN CHIC
LOOK BOOK

_____

What should I wear today?

Photographs
Benoît Peverelli

Direction
Jeanne Le Bault

Flammarion

What should I wear today? It's the same question every day, even with a closet full of clothes. This style guide will help you figure everything out. Especially if you're someone who always says "I have nothing to wear!" Unlike all of the magazines that nudge you to buy new pieces so you can keep up with seasonal trends, these recipes for style show you how to create looks with your own "ingredients"—the clothes you probably already have hanging in your closet.

What's true style? Knowing how to mix the right combinations of ingredients ... and knowing what to do with leftovers. In your closet, you must have a pair of black jeans or blue jeans, a black coat or a trench, a white shirt or a turtleneck, and sandals and boots. That's everything you need to look stylish without embarking on an Olympian shopping spree. Depending on the situation, you might be missing two or three things. But there's no reason to panic, because everything in this guide is totally timeless and can easily be found in any store, from bargain basement to the most luxurious. All of the looks that follow have been created with classic pieces. Of course, you don't need to copy everything to a T, because in fashion, just like in the kitchen, you're allowed to deviate from the recipe.

What should you wear when hosting a dinner party for friends? Should you wear a skirt on a first date? This guide is a kind of perpetual calendar that answers all of your questions for how to have style with minimal effort. You'll soon discover that a white shirt and black pants are all you need to look chic—just like a Parisienne, of course.

....

Ines de la Fressange
Sophie Gachet

The
ESSENTIALS
of
PARISIAN CHIC

We could all spend every day in a T-shirt, jeans, and sneakers. But we'd get bored fast. To avoid filling your closet with clothes you'll never wear, here is a list of the essentials you'll find in any Parisienne's closet.

— Pants, jumpsuits, and shorts

- [ ] Black jeans
- [ ] Raw denim jeans
- [ ] Blue jeans
- [ ] White jeans
- [ ] High-waisted pants
- [ ] Black velvet pants
- [ ] Silk print pants
- [ ] Black cropped pants
- [ ] Black pants
- [ ] Sailor pants
- [ ] Seersucker pants
- [ ] Sweatpants
- [ ] Jumpsuit
- [ ] Denim shorts

— Skirts and dresses

- [ ] Pencil skirt
- [ ] Long skirt
- [ ] Long pleated skirt
- [ ] Simple black dress
- [ ] Long floral-print dress
- [ ] Long shirtdress

— Sweaters, sweatshirts, blouses, and other tops

- [ ] Black turtleneck
- [ ] Black round-neck sweater
- [ ] Beige round-neck sweater
- [ ] Black V-neck sweater
- [ ] Hot pink sweater
- [ ] Chunky knit sweater
- [ ] Gray sweatshirt
- [ ] White ruffled blouse
- [ ] White collarless blouse
- [ ] Plaid shirt
- [ ] Striped shirt
- [ ] Blue shirt
- [ ] White shirt
- [ ] Denim shirt
- [ ] Tank top
- [ ] White T-shirt
- [ ] Black T-shirt
- [ ] Striped sailor shirt
- [ ] Embroidered tunic
- [ ] Long beach tunic
- [ ] Gold top

— Jackets, blazers, and coats

- [ ] Black leather jacket
- [ ] Black blazer
- [ ] Navy blazer
- [ ] Peacoat
- [ ] Windbreaker
- [ ] Ultralight down jacket
- [ ] Tweed jacket
- [ ] Tuxedo jacket
- [ ] Black trench coat
- [ ] Beige trench coat
- [ ] Navy men's overcoat
- [ ] Camel men's overcoat
- [ ] Velvet jacket
- [ ] Bomber jacket
- [ ] Sequined jacket
- [ ] Khaki military jacket
- [ ] Denim jacket
- [ ] Leopard-print coat
- [ ] Shearling coat

— Shoes

- [ ] Penny loafers
- [ ] Patent leather loafers

- ☐ Jeweled flats
- ☐ Black derbies
- ☐ Brown derbies
- ☐ Black platform sandals
- ☐ Black ballet flats
- ☐ Fur-lined boots
- ☐ Black high heels
- ☐ Black kitten heels
- ☐ Black velvet flats
- ☐ Cowboy boots
- ☐ Flat black slide sandals
- ☐ Natural leather sandals
- ☐ Lace-up gladiator sandals
- ☐ Flat gold sandals
- ☐ Lace-up sneakers
- ☐ Slip-on sneakers
- ☐ Gum boots
- ☐ Biker boots
- ☐ Farm and ranch boots

— Bags

- ☐ Saddle bag
- ☐ Mini black evening bag
- ☐ Gold handbag
- ☐ Fringed bag
- ☐ Black handbag
- ☐ Black tote bag
- ☐ Straw tote bag
- ☐ Brown satchel

— Jewelry

- ☐ Cuff bracelet
- ☐ Gold bangles
- ☐ Rhinestone bangles
- ☐ Bracelets
- ☐ Charm necklace
- ☐ Long rhinestone necklace

- ☐ Long pearl necklace
- ☐ Long gold necklace
- ☐ Wooden bead necklace
- ☐ Rhinestone brooches
- ☐ Classic watch
- ☐ Men's watch

— Belts

- ☐ Black belt
- ☐ Brown belt
- ☐ Cummerbund

— Scarves

- ☐ Large shawl
- ☐ Scarf
- ☐ Print foulard
- ☐ Black foulard

— Bathing suits and lingerie

- ☐ Bikini
- ☐ Camisole
- ☐ Black bra
- ☐ Black panties
- ☐ Undies that shouldn't always be kept under wraps …

STYLE IN
A SNAP

How can you transform wardrobe basics into chic looks for any occasion? Here is the Parisienne's dress code and her tried-and-true style recipes.

THE FASHION DILEMMA

"From bed to work in one minute flat"

"Before an appointment at the bank,
I have to manage my assets"

"I have a tricky day ahead"

"Asking for a raise"

"From office to nightclub"

BUSINESS IS BUSINESS

For those who don't wear a
uniform to work, you need
to find an outfit that will
make a good impression
at the office—and we don't
mean one with excessive
(ulterior) motifs!

FROM BED
TO WORK IN
ONE MINUTE FLAT

Ingredients

| Camel men's overcoat

| Black velvet pants

| Black turtleneck

| Black belt

| Biker boots

| Saddle bag

When?

Your alarm didn't go off.

The secret recipe

Play it simple and steer clear of questionable combos. When you don't have time, don't experiment. Stick with chic basics that won't attract the attention of the fashion police. Biker boots loosen up what would otherwise be a rather strict look.

BEFORE AN APPOINTMENT AT THE BANK, I HAVE TO MANAGE MY ASSETS

Ingredients

| Blazer

| Raw denim jeans

| Blue shirt

| Black belt

| Kitten heels

| Handbag

When?

You've overdone it spending on high-end labels and your bank account is in the red. You have to persuade your banker to give you a loan.

The secret recipe

Leave your brand-new clothes in the closet—you don't want your loan officer to figure out where all the money went. To convince him that you're a serious woman who can rein in her expenses, choose a blazer (extra points if it has banker stripes). And to show that your account is not the only thing that's bare, show a little cleavage. Heels are a look you can bank on: if you can rise above it all—even when your account's in the red—you've found the golden ticket for getting out of debt.

I HAVE A TRICKY DAY AHEAD

Ingredients

| Silk print pants

| V-neck sweater

| Black velvet flats

| Rhinestone bangles

| Classic watch

When?

Your day is set to be an endless stream of boring meetings and stressful appointments. Followed by a professional dinner right after work, with no time to pop home in between.

The secret recipe

Arm yourself with clothes that keep you feeling upbeat. Pants with a printed motif immediately make things brighter. Velvet flats will see you through until the wee hours. And if you get bored during a meeting, you can play with your bracelets. Having fun at work is always a recipe for success.

ASKING FOR A RAISE

Ingredients

| Navy blazer

| Blue jeans

| White T-shirt

| Black belt

| Black derbies

| Classic watch

When?

Your coworkers say you shouldn't automatically expect a raise. But you really feel you deserve one.

The secret recipe

If there's ever a time to go totally anti-bling, it's now. You don't need to look like a damsel in distress (your boss knows how much he pays you), but point out to him that you don't intend to spend the rest of your life in loose-fitting jeans and a white T-shirt. Throw in that you're wearing your father's blazer and watch. If he knows anything about fashion, he'll show compassion.

FROM OFFICE
TO NIGHTCLUB

Ingredients

| Tuxedo jacket

| Black cropped pants

| White blouse

| Black bra

| Heels

| Long necklace

When?

There's no time to go home to change into a shiny top before you head out for a night on the town.

The secret recipe

Bet all your chips on the tuxedo jacket: it's chic at the office and sexy at the nightclub. Just take off your blouse and wear nothing under the jacket—Yves Saint Laurent did it before anyone else. Wear the necklace around your neck during the day and as a belt in the evening. Now you're all set to commute, work, and dance.

THE FASHION DILEMMA

"I want to look like Tinderella,
not Barbarella"

"Date night"

"I'm meeting my future in-laws; I want to
look like a catch, not bait"

"I'm meeting his best friend"

"At the courthouse for my divorce"

"My ex has invited me to dinner"

"I'm auditioning for stepmother"

"I'm having lunch with my great-aunt who
hasn't read a fashion magazine since 1970"

"In the sandbox"

"Model mom"

FAMILY AFFAIRS

Between dinner with your
current boyfriend, a date with
a potential one, and a day
at the park with the kids, it's
important not to get your
looks mixed up.

I WANT TO LOOK LIKE TINDERELLA, NOT BARBARELLA

Ingredients

| Tweed jacket

| Raw denim jeans

| Tank top

| Belt

| Heels

When?

Your first date with a potential prince charming. Since he's only seen your face in your profile picture, it's probably best not to reveal too much right away.

The secret recipe

A little tank top for a feminine touch, a tweed blazer for the "traditional + clean-cut" look, tight jeans to avoid looking too guy-ish, a belt to accentuate your waist, and heels to make an impression. As long as you steer clear of a miniskirt and crop top, there's hope.

DATE NIGHT

Ingredients

| Trench coat

| Black bra

| Black panties

| Heels

When?

Your sweetheart asks you to meet him for a drink at the end of the day.

The secret recipe

Just a belted trench coat. Black is best, but if you prefer beige, your man won't object. If you're feeling cold, wear black stockings. With this outfit, you can't fail. And that's an understatement!

I'M MEETING MY FUTURE IN-LAWS; I WANT TO LOOK LIKE A CATCH, NOT BAIT

Ingredients

| Navy blazer

| White jeans

| Striped sailor shirt

| Velvet flats

| Brown satchel

When?

No need to shock them from the get-go; the first time you meet his parents you should make a good impression—better to win them over to your side now.

The secret recipe

If you have time to prepare, roll up the sleeves of your blazer to show you're a girl who's ready for anything. Don't wear heels—they can look haughty. Velvet flats are chic but understated (it's not the time to show your fashion quotient, but rather your "one-man woman" ratio). White pants are the key to this look—they'll give you an innocent, if not angelic air. Just right for melting the hearts of your future in-laws.

I'M MEETING HIS BEST FRIEND

Ingredients

| Navy men's overcoat

| White jeans

| Denim shirt

| Brown belt

| Brown derbies

When?

To make the right impression on your boyfriend's best buddy. As with the in-laws, it would be wise to have this influencer in the palm of your hand.

The secret recipe

Avoid looking like a tease to reassure this pal who has your man's best interests at heart. The denim shirt is a good choice as it's a garment he could wear himself. He'll think his friend has finally found a woman who holds up, and one who feels comfortable in her own skin. Even when fully dressed.

AT THE COURTHOUSE FOR MY DIVORCE

Ingredients

| Black blazer

| White jeans

| Beige round-neck sweater

| Black belt

| Penny loafers

| Saddle bag

When?

If the judge still hasn't realized that your ex-husband is lowballing his income to avoid paying alimony.

The secret recipe

White for innocence, beige for sweetness, a blazer for seriousness, college loafers to convey the message of student-level income. No jewelry, of course. A saddle bag will show you are not the kind of woman to blow your money on an It Bag.

MY EX HAS INVITED ME TO DINNER

Ingredients

| Velvet jacket

| Pencil skirt

| Camisole

| Heels

| Classic watch

When?

You haven't seen each other for years and out of the blue your ex invites you to dinner. Now's your chance to show him what he's been missing.

The secret recipe

Steer clear of the "vamp for grabs" look and choose a subtler weapon of seduction: the pencil skirt. Don't wear a suggestive low-cut top—we said "subtle seduction." A silk lace camisole will do the trick, and if he remarks that it's a little sexy, just reply, "I'm not going to be out late, I'll be off to bed soon." Don't carry a handbag: this will prove you didn't bring a toothbrush or a change of clothes, if ever he thought he still had a chance.

I'M AUDITIONING FOR STEPMOTHER

Ingredients

| Raw denim jeans

| Striped shirt

| Black belt

| Jeweled flats

| Charm necklace

When?

For your first meeting with your future stepchildren, you need to get off on the right foot. Somewhere between mother and girlfriend is what you're aiming for.

The secret recipe

Forget about being seductive (that can be scary for children). Choose neutral shades, except for your shoes, which can be embroidered with jewels, topped with pompoms, gold, or sequined (even at lunchtime) to show you have no intention of playing the evil stepmother and that you're there to have fun.

I'M HAVING LUNCH WITH MY GREAT-AUNT

WHO HASN'T READ A FASHION MAGAZINE SINCE 1970

Ingredients

| High-waisted pants

| Ruffled blouse

| Platform sandals

| Foulard

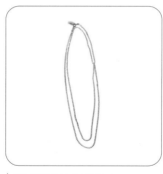

| Rhinestone necklace

When?

You're meeting an older person who's no longer interested in fashion.

The secret recipe

Paradoxically, this is when you can be a real fashion victim, because everything your great-aunt loved in the 1970s is back in style today. With high-waisted pants, a ruffled blouse, a foulard worn as a belt, and platform sandals, she'll think you're fabulous—without realizing you're actually at the cutting edge of style.

IN THE SANDBOX

Ingredients

| Trench coat

| Blue jeans

| Hot pink sweater

| Ballet flats

| Men's watch

| Straw tote bag

When?

People with kids know the playground is prison for parents. Considering all the pitfalls in such a place, it's best to be comfortably dressed if you have to babysit your nephews, nieces, or godchildren.

The secret recipe

Choose jeans in resistant indigo fabric, recommended for dealing with unforeseen events during a day at the park. A hot pink sweater can be hard to find in stores, but it's reassuring for children as they'll feel they can't lose you in the crowd. Plus it'll flatter your complexion. And wear ballet flats—we've all seen mothers wearing high heels on the playground, and it just doesn't work!

MODEL MOM

Ingredients

| Navy men's overcoat

| Blue jeans

| Gray sweatshirt

| Black belt

| Lace-up sneakers

| Saddle bag

When?

When school gets out. You want to look like you know the score, but the only time you've been here was on the first day of school.

The secret recipe

Don't show up with a fancy handbag; you'll look like the kind of mom who doesn't know your kids need a snack after school. Your uniform should be jeans, sweatshirt, and sneakers, because you might have to run to keep up with your kids in the park.

THE FASHION DILEMMA

"Calamity (not plain) Jane"

"Coachella, even though it's Shakespeare in the Park"

"Which way to the sea?"

"The Love Boat"

"Garden party, without going full bloom"

"Me Jane, you Tarzan"

"I love leather and rock'n'roll"

"Say it with flowers"

KEY PIECES

There are clothes and accessories that can create a whole look in themselves—or break it, if you don't know how to wear them. Fringe, leopard prints, and sailor shirts may abound, but there's no need to get on your high horse, pull out your claws, or rock the boat to create your look.

CALAMITY (NOT PLAIN) JANE

Ingredients

| Brown fringed bag

| White jeans

| Blue shirt

| Black belt

| Cowboy boots

| Men's watch

When?

Because you like a fringed bag. And to show your man you can be (quite) wild. Or simply to amuse the kids.

The secret recipe

Fringe should always be used with a neutral background. White, black, gray, and beige are allowed. No flashy colors with fringed accessories, unless you want to relive Woodstock 1969. Tassels and fringe prove you could sleep in a tipi, à la Pocahontas. With that you're already stylin'.

COACHELLA, EVEN THOUGH IT'S SHAKESPEARE IN THE PARK

Ingredients

| Denim shorts

| White T-shirt

| Brown belt

| Farm and ranch boots

| Fringed bag

| Foulard

| Cuff bracelet

When?

You want to dig out those denim shorts at last. Or you're after a bohemian chic style but don't want to be mistaken for a harpy hippie. The perfect excuse: a sunny outdoor festival.

The secret recipe

It takes a bit of attitude to pull off wearing denim shorts. Obviously there's an age limit, and we'll let you be the judge of that. Sometimes a cotton peasant skirt can also do the trick, if the idea of denim shorts terrifies you. In all cases, farm and ranch boots are de rigueur. Never mind if it's scorching hot outside—sometimes you have to suffer to be cool. Wear the foulard as a bracelet, and if you have a fringed bag, now's the time to use it.

WHICH WAY TO THE SEA?

Ingredients

| Striped sailor shirt

| Raw denim jeans

| Navy peacoat

| Lace-up sneakers

| Rhinestone brooch

When?

You feel like wearing your sailor shirt, and who cares if some people think you're off to go clam digging.

The secret recipe

You're aiming for nautical style (with striped sailor shirt and peacoat), without looking like a cabin boy. Instead of rubber boots, wear sneakers and—to minimize the salty dog look—wear a rhinestone brooch. We call that glam rigging.

THE LOVE BOAT

Ingredients

| Sailor pants

| Tuxedo jacket

| White shirt

| Flat slide sandals

| Mini evening bag

When?

You have sea legs and want to expand your horizons.

The secret recipe

Sailor pants have that chic je ne sais quoi. The must accessories are flat slide sandals and a mini evening bag; this will tone down the naval look. Add rhinestones anywhere you want; it'll be brilliant.

GARDEN PARTY, WITHOUT GOING FULL BLOOM

Ingredients

| Seersucker pants

| Ruffled blouse

| Natural leather sandals

| Pearl necklace

| Straw tote bag

When?

It's been far too long since you last wore your seersucker pants. That's true, you never get the chance to wear them!

The secret recipe

Skip the cheesy floral-print dress you're tempted to bring out for any garden gathering. The alternative? Seersucker pants are extremely lightweight, so they're perfect for the occasion. Add a white ruffled blouse for an even fresher look. For a bucolic touch, there's the straw tote—and to chase away the country bumpkin effect, wear a pearl necklace as a belt.

ME JANE,
YOU TARZAN

Ingredients

| Leopard-print coat

| White jeans

| Black round-neck sweater

| Black belt

| Black derbies

When?

Your animal instinct spurs you to buy a leopard-print coat.

The secret recipe

Although magazines try to persuade us that the head-to-toe animal look is all the rage, taming the wild with understated pieces seems a more reasonable approach to us. Choose between white or black pants and a black or white sweater, but avoid bringing out the beast with loud shades.

I LOVE LEATHER AND ROCK'N'ROLL

Ingredients

| Black leather jacket

| Black jeans

| White shirt

| Black belt

| Black derbies

When?

Occasionally, upon spying our leather jacket in the closet, we suddenly have a Rolling Stones moment.

The secret recipe

Think of the dress code for sexiness and do just the opposite. No skirt with a leather jacket. No low-cut neckline with a leather jacket. And no heels with a leather jacket either. That's what being a Rolling Stone is all about.

SAY IT WITH FLOWERS

Ingredients

| Plaid shirt

| Floral-print dress

| Brown belt

| Farm and ranch boots

When?

Because we never know how to wear that plaid shirt, which always has a "walk in the woods" air about it.

The secret recipe

Think of what a lumberjack wouldn't do. For example, he wouldn't wear his shirt with a floral print dress. And voilà—that's just the right combo to feminize this rustic look. Complete it with a leather belt to retain the country feel. And to avoid all sappiness, wear suede boots. Wow, that was hard work!

THE FASHION DILEMMA

"Cocktail arty"

"My cousin Audrey"

"Dinner in a hip restaurant"

"Dinner at home with friends"

"A dinner with no dress code"

"A friend's birthday party"

"Girls' night out"

"Saturday Night Fever"

"Dinner on the dunes"

"It's Christmas!"

"New Year's Eve—it's showtime"

EVENING WEAR

The LBD is, of course, our go-to garment for any evening event. But if you want to stray a little from the beaten path, what should you wear at night to look festive (but not decked out in your Sunday best)?

COCKTAIL ARTY

Ingredients

| Black leather jacket

| Silk print pants

| White shirt

| Flat slide sandals

| Black handbag

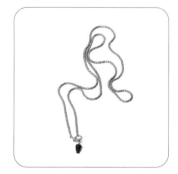

| Long gold necklace

When?

An art exhibition opening.

The secret recipe

Obviously, you can always dig out your most beautiful top-label print dress and pass yourself off as a fashion work of art. At this type of event, however, it's best to keep a low profile. Black and white will always create a graphic effect, and wearing a necklace as a bracelet is creative. Who said fashion isn't an art?

MY COUSIN AUDREY

Ingredients

| Black dress

| Kitten heels

| Mini evening bag

| Rhinestone brooches

When?

Sometimes we end up at some ceremony or another and have no idea how or why we're there. Whether it's the opening of a button store or your cousin's cousin's charity gala, these events require sartorial thought.

The secret recipe

Take inspiration from Audrey Hepburn, the queen of the little black dress. Invest in sparkly accessories (lamé, sequined, or rhinestones) that will keep any outfit from looking too understated. The LBD is a fabulous invention: if it's simple, you can wear it for a myriad of different occasions, since no one ever remembers a little black dress. By dressing it up with rhinestone brooches, you can make it look precious. And wearing your handbag chain as a bracelet makes the bag doubly useful.

DINNER IN A HIP RESTAURANT

Ingredients

| Tuxedo jacket

| Black pants

| White shirt

| Black foulard

| Black velvet flats

When?

You're invited out to that hip restaurant everyone's talking about, but you have no idea what is considered a hip outfit these days (it's always changing!).

The secret recipe

"Less is more" fashion. The less you show off labels and the less you try and sum up the season's details in one outfit, the better the result will be. Black and white always make for a totally flawless look, even in a trendy crowd. If you feel daring, tie the foulard at your collar. And if you're asked where you got the pussy bow blouse, reply cooly, "It's an idea of my own, but I think Yves Saint Laurent may have thought of it, too."

DINNER AT HOME
WITH FRIENDS

Ingredients

| Blue jeans

| White blouse

| Black belt

| Gold bangles

| Black velvet flats

When?

You've invited friends over for dinner and don't want them to feel they should have made an effort to dress up.

The secret recipe

Wear a slightly chic top but casual pants. That way, your friends will feel comfortable no matter how they've turned up. Whatever happens, make sure you wear mascara—you'll get points for looking chic without overdoing it.

A DINNER WITH NO DRESS CODE

Ingredients

| Black tuxedo jacket

| Black pants

| Black T-shirt

| Black heels

| Black handbag

When?

You're invited to a dinner and you don't know anyone.

The secret recipe

Wager everything on black, the color everyone can agree on. When you don't know any-one, you don't want to arrive overdressed, or—even worse—underdressed. So wear black only and steer clear of slogan prints (a militant T-shirt can ruin your evening). The "No Look" is the perfect illustration of "less is more."

A FRIEND'S BIRTHDAY PARTY

Ingredients

| Bomber jacket

| Pencil skirt

| Gold top

| Heels

When?

Your friend's having a birthday party but she hasn't asked anyone to come in costume.

The secret recipe

Looking cheery for a birthday party is the best gift you can give your friend. A gold top will do the trick. To avoid the "holiday" look, pair it with a bomber jacket. And because a birthday is an official celebration, the pencil skirt adds a solemn touch.

GIRLS' NIGHT OUT

Ingredients

| Jumpsuit

| White T-shirt

| Flat gold sandals

| Gold handbag

When?

An evening out with the girls—no men allowed.

The secret recipe

This is the time to wear anything you please! Guys never like jumpsuits. We, however, love the mechanic look. Wear flats, because there are a few men who find jumpsuits sexy with heels. This night out is not about being seductive. Make the most of it and wear tons of gloss—guys hate sticky lips.

SATURDAY NIGHT FEVER

Ingredients

| Black pants

| Gold top

| Patent leather loafers

| Mini evening bag with
| cross-strap

When?

In a nightclub. You're going out in search of your soul mate (it could happen in a night-club) or to chaperone your eighteen-year-old.

The secret recipe

Avoid looking like John Travolta in a white suit—it's a fine look, but it's all been seen and done before. The disco touch is in the gold top. It'll give oafs out cruising the chance to say, "Wow, you must be good as gold." And don't bother wearing heels: you need flats to dance all night. Even Cinderella couldn't make it past midnight in heels.

DINNER ON THE DUNES

Ingredients

| Long dress

| Black pants

| Lace-up gladiator sandals

| Straw tote bag

| Bracelets

When?

In southern climes, when a well-intentioned friend invites you to picnic on the beach.

The secret recipe

Think of a gypsy in a big flowing dress. But to keep mosquitoes at bay, wear pants under the dress. In the tote, bring a big shawl that can be useful in a multitude of ways—such as keeping the chill off if you don't end up roasting marshmallows over an open fire.

IT'S CHRISTMAS!

Ingredients

| Long pleated skirt

| Hot pink sweater

| Cummerbund

| Ballet flats

| Rhinestone bracelets

| Rhinestone brooch

When?

Christmas Eve.

The secret recipe

Do away with the usual "dress + jewelry everywhere" look! The hot pink top conveys the festive spirit. You'll look glamorous with the long flowing skirt and a tad casual with the ballerina flats—you're with the family, after all. For sparkle, deck yourself out in rhinestones. And be joyful, it's Christmas!

NEW YEAR'S EVE— IT'S SHOWTIME

Ingredients

| Sequined jacket

| White jeans

| White T-shirt

| Heels

| Gold and rhinestone bangles

When?

To ring in the New Year with good cheer.

The secret recipe

Whoopee, you can finally wear all the sequins you want without anyone saying, ironically, "Wow, look who's channeling New Year's Eve!" Wear white for this night out. If you're asked why, simply say, "It's a tradition in Brazil." After all, having experienced many a New Year's Eve party, you've learned one thing: party attire is really just a state of mind.

THE FASHION DILEMMA

"Next stop: the airport!"

"The beach is the new red carpet"

"Country chic on Saturday"

"Down-to-earth rustic on Sunday"

"Sunny day BBQ"

"Beach party"

"A Passage to India"

"A dinner in the mountains without
going off-piste"

"Visiting the Eiffel Tower"

VACATION TIME

Whether you're off for a weekend in the country or a vacation by the sea, you need to pack the right ingredients in your suitcase.

NEXT STOP: THE AIRPORT!

Ingredients

| Navy men's overcoat

| Sweatpants

| T-shirt

| V-neck sweater

| Flat slide sandals

When?

When flying.

The secret recipe

Even if you're only taking a thirty-minute short hop, act as though you're crossing the Atlantic. The idea is to blend casual comfort (sweatpants and slides) with sophisticated pieces (the men's overcoat). Put on sweatpants and forget about your jeans (even if you're slim, jeans leave marks). Skip the jewelry, belts, and anything else that sets off the metal detectors. Wear comfy shoes—not only is it easier to kick them off, but wearing slides, which are almost like slippers, in the plane will give you a touch of (business) class.

THE BEACH IS THE NEW RED CARPET

Ingredients

| Bikini

| Long beach tunic

| Belt

| Bracelets

| Straw tote bag

| Natural leather sandals

When?

Whenever you hit the sand—from Miami Beach to South Mission Beach, Crompton Bay to Botany Bay, or Bondi Beach to Byron Bay Beach—dress as if you were walking a red carpet.

The secret recipe

All too often we mistakenly think that a swimsuit is all you need at the seaside. Not at all. It should be worn with all sorts of accessories, to keep it from looking like just any old bathing suit. If you want to make waves, layer necklaces and bracelets. And belt your tunic—just because you're at the beach, it doesn't mean you should let your style get stuck in the sand.

COUNTRY CHIC
ON SATURDAY

Ingredients

| Khaki military jacket

| Long floral-print dress

| Chunky knit sweater

| Belt

| Gum boots

When?

You're meeting friends in a big house on the prairie.

The secret recipe

In honor of the Ingalls family, wear a floral-print dress. If you know you're going to encounter animals, leave your favorite jeans and this season's new boots in your closet. Instead, pull out your wellies, ideal boots for dealing with any kind of weather or animal. Add the military jacket for a "country chic" look.

DOWN-TO-EARTH RUSTIC ON SUNDAY

Ingredients

| Peacoat

| Blue jeans

| Gray sweatshirt

| Chunky knit sweater

| Gum boots

When?

After you've spent a day on the prairie herding cattle, sheep, and pigs, your flowery dress might not look quite so fresh.

The secret recipe

For this second day in the country, you'll tone down the chic for a more down-to-earth look. Jeans are perfect. Pull on a sweatshirt (it's always a little bit chilly) and throw the chunky sweater over your shoulders, just in case. With your rubber boots, you can slosh around in the mud until the cows come home.

SUNNY DAY
BBQ

Ingredients

| Striped shirt

| Camisole

| Denim shorts

| Natural leather sandals

| Men's watch

When?

A barbecue at your favorite vacation spot.

The secret recipe

A relaxed meal calls for relaxed attire, but certain rules still apply. That's why you should always avoid the T-shirt pitfall that immediately screams "I'm not making an effort for a barbecue lunch." Wearing a camisole top to chow down on chargrilled sausages is just the kind of offbeat look we love.

BEACH PARTY

Ingredients

| Long shirtdress

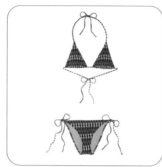

| Bikini

| Denim shorts

| Lace-up gladiator sandals

| Wooden bead necklace

When?

You're off on a trip to an island where partying is the number one activity.

The secret recipe

Wear your bikini all day long, with denim shorts that you can pull off easily and a shirt-dress. When you go out in the evening, you can take off the shorts—a look that will see you through to the midnight swim.

A PASSAGE TO INDIA

Ingredients

| Embroidered tunic

| Long skirt

| Brown belt

| Lace-up gladiator sandals

| Gold bangles

| Cuff bracelet

When?

You're nowhere near India but have a sudden craving for curry.

The secret recipe

Spicing up your style with a traditional embroidered tunic will make people think you've traveled far afield to find your look. This is the perfect opportunity to layer your jewelry—in the summer, you don't have to worry about being mistaken for a Christmas tree. Venturing into foreign territories will immediately turn you into the Indiana Jones of fashion.

A DINNER IN THE MOUNTAINS WITHOUT GOING OFF-PISTE

Ingredients

| Shearling coat

| Denim jacket

| White jeans

| Chunky knit sweater

| Fur-lined boots

| Scarf

When?

On a winter sports vacation, when you need to look like a fashion champ but you're stuck in snow.

The secret recipe

There is no way you're going out in a ski suit—even if it's sub-freezing outside. Looking sexy on the beach is par for the course, but on the slopes it's so much hotter. Here's how to combine warmth and sensuality: you have to layer, so you can peel each one off as the temperature rises. Sometimes you just need to play it cool.

VISITING THE EIFFEL TOWER

Ingredients

| Peacoat

| Blue jeans

| Round-neck sweater

| Lace-up sneakers

| Saddle bag

When?

For a visit to the Eiffel Tower, whether you're a true Parisienne or not.

The secret recipe

For those who are not Parisian, don't think you have to sport your trendiest outfit to measure up to the locals. *Au contraire*, it's precisely by not making too much of an effort that you'll look most like a genuine Parisienne. Choose relaxed, comfortable clothes: jeans and especially sneakers, since you'll need to walk up all those stairs to get to the top of the Eiffel Tower (that way, you'll skip the long line for the elevators).

THE FASHION DILEMMA

—————

"Normcore with a sparkle"

"Very, very simple"

"Effortless chic"

"For hardcore shopping"

"Singing in the rain"

"Oh baby it's cold out there"

"Museum buff"

EXTRA-SPECIAL OCCASIONS

There will be times when you really have no idea what to wear, when simply peering into your closet makes you want to go back to bed. Especially if it's raining outside. Don't despair—even in these moments, there is a solution.

NORMCORE WITH
A SPARKLE

Ingredients

| Trench coat

| Sequined jacket

| Blue jeans

| Blue shirt

| Lace-up sneakers

When?

You're after a simple look with a touch of glam.

The secret recipe

What could be simpler than a trench coat + jeans + blue shirt + sneakers? This outfit will see you through any situation. And if you're stepping out in the evening, don't forget the sequined jacket—paired with sneakers, it'll really shine.

VERY, VERY SIMPLE

Ingredients

| Navy blazer

| Raw denim jeans

| Gray sweatshirt

| Black derbies

| Saddle bag

When?

If you're feeling uninspired, this should be your go-to outfit.

The secret recipe

Ok, it may be super-simple, but we like looks that have something obvious about them—those that prove you're not trying to be trendy, no matter what. Even if you do wear a blazer with a sweatshirt. If anyone asks, we call this look casual cool.

EFFORTLESS CHIC

Ingredients

| Peacoat

| Black velvet pants

| Ruffled blouse

| Platform sandals

When?

Anytime. Although obviously for any situation when high heels won't be over-the-top.

The secret recipe

You don't need to wear spectacular pieces to look sophisticated. Silk and velvet, in classic shapes, will provide you with the perfect appearance. The peacoat, with its utilitarian connotations, gives the style an "effortless" tone. Unless, of course, you're at the harbor and get asked to tug a few lines.

FOR HARDCORE SHOPPING

Ingredients

| Jumpsuit

| T-shirt

| Slip-on sneakers

| Tote bag

When?

For a hardcore shopping marathon, so you don't have to spend your whole day undressing and redressing in the fitting room.

The secret recipe

Mechanic overalls are practical, especially when it's not just the oil that needs a quick change. Carry an oversize tote bag for your purchases so you don't end up looking like a porter with tons of shopping bags. Free yourself of any time-wasting constraints like complicated bras or lace-up shoes. If it were up to you, you'd hit the sales in your undies!

SINGING IN THE RAIN

Ingredients

| Trench coat

| Windbreaker

| Black cropped pants

| Round-neck sweater

| Penny loafers

When?

For a rainy day.

The secret recipe

Who said windbreakers were only for kids? You'd think that the trench coat was the ultimate raincoat, but it doesn't keep you as warm as a good windbreaker. So wear one under your trench coat to keep out the chill. And if your windbreaker has a hood, you can burn your umbrella. Even old ladies find them inconvenient.

OH BABY IT'S COLD OUT THERE

Ingredients

| Leather jacket

| Ultralight down jacket

| Velvet pants

| Turtleneck sweater

| Fur-lined boots

| Saddle bag

When?

When the temperature drops and you're on foot.

The secret recipe

Save your oversize down jacket for skiing. In the city, wear an ultralight one under a warm jacket. Keeping out the chill doesn't mean you have to look like a walking quilt.

MUSEUM BUFF

Ingredients

| Denim jacket

| Black dress

| Lace-up sneakers

| Rhinestone bracelets

| Saddle bag

When?

For exhibition-hopping without losing any of your fashion savvy.

The secret recipe

Wear your black dress—the grand dame of fashion history—with a denim jacket, that pretty young thing from the twentieth century. For a modern touch, add sneakers—perfect for walking around all of those exhibitions—and a colorful bag for a dash of the artistic. Don't be surprised if you're asked to stay in the museum as a fashionable work of art.

20
FASHION
FAUX
PAS

The world of fashion is constantly changing, so it's difficult to make a list of all the dos and don'ts. Everything can shift from one day to the next, and the fashion flops of today could well become the musts of tomorrow. Yet there are some things that the Parisienne simply can't bring herself to wear. Here's the lowdown on what to avoid, unless you want to have a run-in with the fashion police.

Leggings

Unless you're eleven and taking dance lessons, leggings do not look good on anyone. They are tolerable with a very long, chunky sweater, but it's a typical lounging outfit and one we highly recommend you keep at home.

———

The knockoff bag

There's nothing stylish about carrying a bag that's an imitation of a well-known brand. Putting aside the conditions under which it was made and its mediocre quality, the bag is much less luxurious than a genuine and sincere cotton tote bag.

———

Bermuda shorts with pockets

Ok, so you've never worn a pair. But you never know, you could be tempted to try them one day as a change from denim shorts. Make no mistake: no designer worthy of the name has ever put this garment on the runway. That's a sign.

———

PLATFORM SNEAKERS

They might be super-trendy at times, but they will always remain clunky shoes that make for ungainly feet. Even on women with slender legs.

Culottes

We recommend these pant skirts to any woman who wants to go out without being hassled or who's seeking an amicable separation from her husband.

Long down jackets

When it comes to down jackets there are two possibilities: either an ultralight one that you slip on under your overcoat, or a short bulky one that you wear to go skiing. A long jacket stuffed with feathers will give you a swollen figure. Which is fine if you're vying for a job as the mascot of a tire manufacturer.

————

Head-to-toe fur

Skip it, unless you think Cruella is chic.

Crepe-soled shoes

————

These are an absolute no-no if you wish to avoid adding twenty years to your age with one pair of shoes.

———

Ventilated plastic clogs (Crocs)

They may be sold by the thousands but we'll never like them—even if they're for a three-year-old and are to be worn indoors at the daycare center (they do come in handy for painting classes). We must resist them. Style is something you can't learn early enough.

———

Bras with clear straps

Parisiennes are highly allergic to these. We still don't get why women who wear them think others won't notice the plastic straps. If you really want to look like you're not wearing a bra, just don't wear one.

———

The total designer look

If there's one thing the Parisian woman condemns it's not knowing how to come up with your own look and copying everything from a designer's catalog. God may be a creator, but don't sacrifice your style to one who is certainly not God.

———

THE LITTLE
CAT T-SHIRT

———————

This is fine as long as
you're not yet in middle
school. Any older and you'll
look ridiculous. And a kitty
print probably won't have
the guys purring over you.
For that, a feline print
is a safer bet.

Piling on the jewelry

Earrings with a necklace, rings, and bracelets? Sorry, there is surely one, if not two items too many there. You can, of course, layer your jewelry, but only in one spot. The days when women sought to establish their power with their jewelry collection are over. Especially if it's costume jewelry. Remember to remove one accessory before you leave the house—you'll still be sufficiently adorned.

Flesh-colored stockings

As with the aforementioned clear bra straps, who do you think will believe your skin is that velvety? Nude stockings are far from being invisible, and on top of that they don't keep you warm. Wear black ones.

The spandex bustier

This is never a good idea. First, because items in 100% spandex should be exclusively reserved for the gym. And because if the bustier is slightly too small, you'll be catapulted directly into the realm of the vulgar. Decidedly not chic.

Showing too much skin

It doesn't take much: just wear a T-shirt that's too short and a miniskirt, and in a flash you'll have that reality TV look.

———

Very low hip-huggers

These give everyone a glimpse of your undies or thong. No need to explain what's wrong with that.

———

A mix of stripes

You see this in fashion magazines, but outside the glossies, stripes that run into one another don't create an attractive line.

———

The bucket hat

This really isn't the best hat. If you want to cover your head, try a sailor cap.

Mom jeans

Said like this, they sound cool. The problem is, mom jeans look far too relaxed. Like you've let yourself go, to be honest. From time to time, the hip and trendy bring them back into the spotlight, but as we tend to run from trends, this is certainly not one we'd make an exception for—they give you a hopelessly shapeless figure.

FASHIONABLE STYLE TRICKS

Being stylish sometimes comes down to the details: the smallest twist can earn a lot of fashion points. Here are twenty offbeat tricks to ensure you always look like a fashion pro.

....

#1
Pair a straw bag with an evening dress

#2
Cinch your blazer with two belts

#3
Buy clothes in the men's department

#4
Roll up the hem of your jeans and wear them with heels

#5
Turn your V-neck backward for a bare-back look

#6
Use a ribbon as a belt

#7
Pair fuchsia socks with derbies

#8
Wear a tuxedo jacket
with sneakers

#9
Sport a motorcycle jacket
with a chiffon dress

#10
Cut out the collars
of your T-shirts

#11
Wear a sparkly scarf
with jeans

#12
Add a rhinestone
necklace over a chunky
wool sweater

#13
Wear a pencil skirt
with a windbreaker

#14
Tie a foulard around your
neck, like a dog collar

#15
Wear a khaki military
jacket over a little
black dress

#16
Pair leopard-print shoes
with a gold handbag

#17
Wear a denim jacket
with velvet pants

#18
Use a pearl necklace
as a belt

#19
Wear a rock T-shirt
with a pencil skirt

#20
Pair an embroidered
tunic with tuxedo pants

CHARM WITH STYLE

In fashionable matters you should remain polite at all times. If someone comments on your look, here are a few replies that are 100% Parisienne.

....

"That's such a pretty sweater."

Reply: "Thanks, but it's old!"
Translation: "I bought it two weeks ago."

....

"Aren't those heels killing you?"

Reply: "No, I feel like I'm in slippers."
Translation: "I've been wearing them at home for three weeks with thick wool socks."

"Aren't you cold in that?"

Reply: "Not at all, camisoles keep you warm."

Translation: "I'm not waiting until July to look sexy."

"Your pants are the perfect cut."

Reply: "I bought them for next to nothing in a discount store."

Translation: "I needed a loan to buy these pricey pants."

"Wow, your diamond necklace is fabulous!"

Reply: "These are fakes, but they do the trick."

Translation: "These ten-carat diamonds belonged to my grandmother, but had she known I would be wearing them with a denim shirt, she would never have given them to me."

MY S.O.S. STYLES

Jot down your favorite looks so you can copy them in an emergency.

SHOPPING LIST

Are you missing key items in your closet? Note them down, below. You must deserve a present for something, right? It's essential, it just can't wait!

INDEX BY SITUATION

VACATION TIME

EXTRA-SPECIAL OCCASIONS

INDEX
BY ITEM

ACKNOWLEDGMENTS

Benoît Peverelli, our test pilot for the "Girls' Night Out" look, who is a top photographer and model father.

Rodolphe Bricard, our test pilot for the "Date Night" look, who broke the record for the most photos shot in the least amount of time.

Johanna Scher, who doesn't need our help to dress in the morning. She deserves the Oscar for best producer.

Jean-Louis Bergamini, the quiet force behind the production.

Armelle Saint-Mleux, the brain, who even knows how to "repost" photos on Instagram.

Olga, brilliant in every role.

Laura de Lucia who was beyond reproach throughout, even when assisting Benoît . . .

Alexandra Kan, who holds the secret to bulking us up five pounds in one photo shoot ("foie gras and Nutella" method).

Jeanne Le Bault, a genius stylist (top designers agree).

Marie-Aline Boussagnol, the stylish queen of Snapchat who wields a mean garment steamer.

Marielle Loubet, a hair and makeup angel who know how to bring out your best for a Tinder date.

Elisabeth Serve, a stylist for whom folding clothes is an art.

Sabine, a seamstress who can turn a bikini into a museum-quality work of art.

Marla, a Bordeaux beauty whose legendary smile never leaves her face, even when told her head will be guillotined.

Fanny, who'll become a supermodel without us. Or maybe with us for a future book.

Dinky, who contributed to the great ambiance on the set and who behaved like a (top) model dog.